AMAZING BIRDS

FUN FACTS
AND
ACTIVITIES FOR CURIOUS KIDS

SL PUBLISHING

WELCOME TO THE WORLD OF BIRDS!

Did you know not all birds sound the same? Some chirp, some whistle, some squawk, and some can even copy sounds like car alarms or human voices.

Birds have been around since the time of the dinosaurs, and they've been living alongside people for thousands of years.

Today, you can find birds almost everywhere. Soaring over oceans, nesting in forests, waddling across icy lands, and even singing in your own backyard.

A bird isn't just a pretty singer, it's also an expert traveler and explorer. From tiny hummingbirds to giant eagles and speedy falcons, all birds have special beaks, feathers, and super senses that help them survive in their habitats.

Birds are amazing animals. They can fly across entire continents, build intricate nests, and some can even sleep while gliding through the sky.

So grab your curiosity and look up. Let's discover the feathery, fluttering, and totally awesome world of birds, from the smallest songbirds to the biggest flyers!

BIRDS...WHAT ARE THEY?

Blue Waxbills

Birds are animals that have feathers, wings, and are warm-blooded, which means their bodies stay about the same temperature even when it is hot or cold outside.

There are around 10,000 different kinds, or species, of birds in the world, from tiny hummingbirds to huge ostriches.

Common Chaffinch

Some birds can fly very high and very far, but others, like penguins and ostriches, are called flightless birds because they cannot fly at all.

Birds have hollow bones, which makes their skeletons strong but light, helping many of them fly more easily.

Birds use songs and calls to communicate. They may sing to find a mate, warn others of danger, or tell other birds to stay out of their space.

Birds are important helpers in nature because they spread seeds, pollinate some plants, and eat insects and other pests that might harm crops and gardens.

Birds are vertebrates, which means they have a backbone inside their body, just like people, dogs, and fish do.

Long ago, during the time of the dinosaurs, there were reptiles that looked a little like birds and a little like lizards, and scientists think birds came from these dinosaur like reptiles.

When many dinosaurs died out at the end of the dinosaur era, some small, feathered dinosaur birds survived, and those survivors slowly became the many kinds of birds we see today.

Ancient Egyptian carving of birds in papyrus plants along the Nile River.

In ancient civilizations such as Egypt, Greece, and Rome, certain birds, like doves, geese, and songbirds, were kept in homes and temples, blurring the line between useful animals, sacred symbols, and early pets.

Very early humans hunted birds and gathered their eggs for food, and archaeologists have found ancient sites with bird bones and tools together, showing that people were using birds as resources deep in prehistory.

An Image of a bird hunter/fowler carrying captured birds in Nebamun's tomb in Thebes

WHAT DO BIRDS EAT?

Sun conure parrots

Birds don't have teeth. Their beaks are shaped to match the foods they eat. Some birds have sharp, hooked beaks for tearing meat; thin, pointy beaks for picking up insects; or thick, strong beaks for cracking seeds.

Because birds swallow their food in chunks, many have a strong organ called a gizzard that grinds up the food, it sometimes does this with the help of grit or small stones the bird swallows.

Many seed eating birds use their beaks like little nutcrackers, crushing hard seed shells so they can get to the soft, tasty part inside.

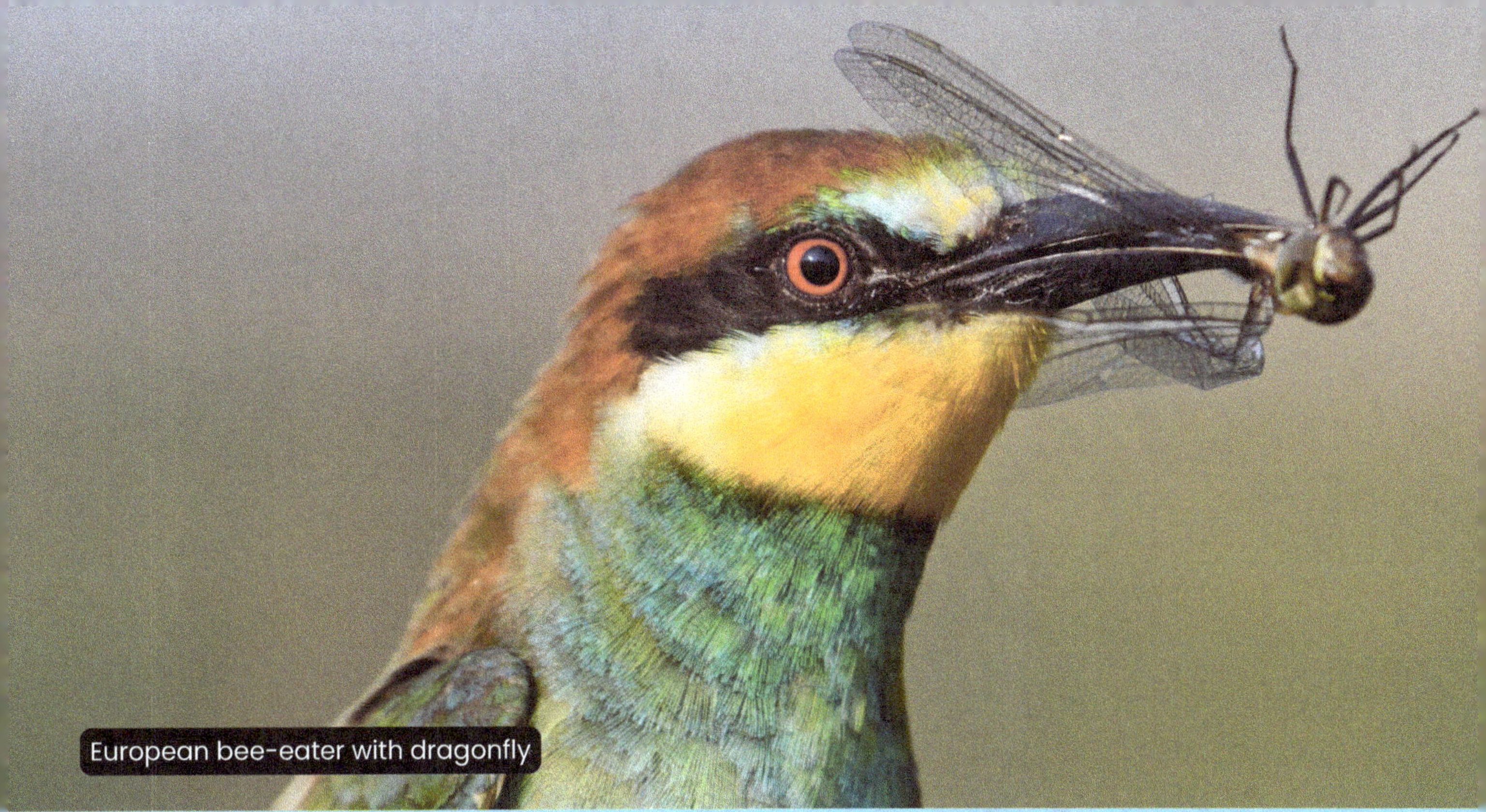

European bee-eater with dragonfly

Insect-eating birds often snatch bugs right out of the air or off leaves and bark, moving quickly so the insects can't escape.

Birds that drink nectar, like hummingbirds, have long, narrow beaks and special tongues that can reach deep into flowers to sip the sweet liquid.

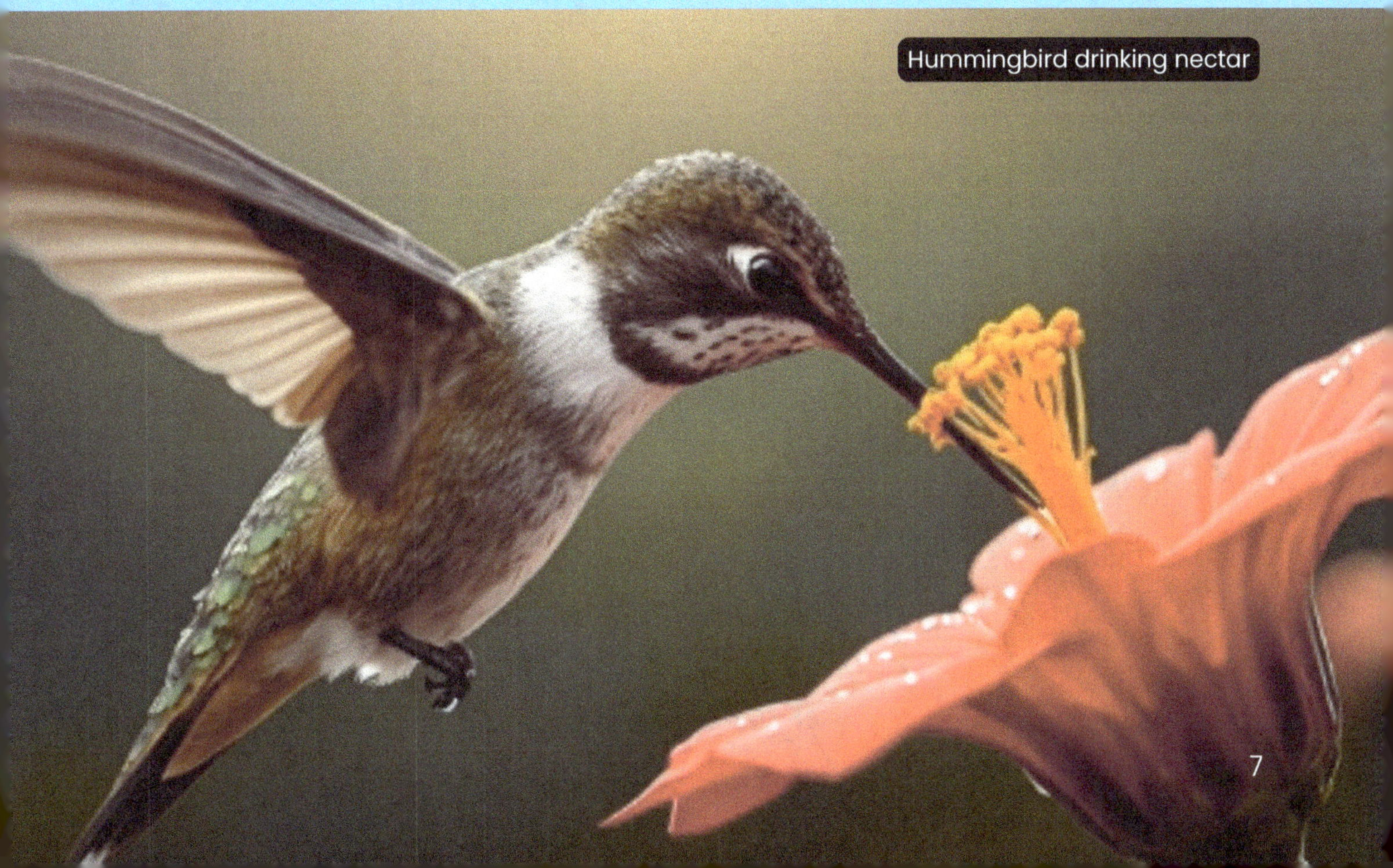

Hummingbird drinking nectar

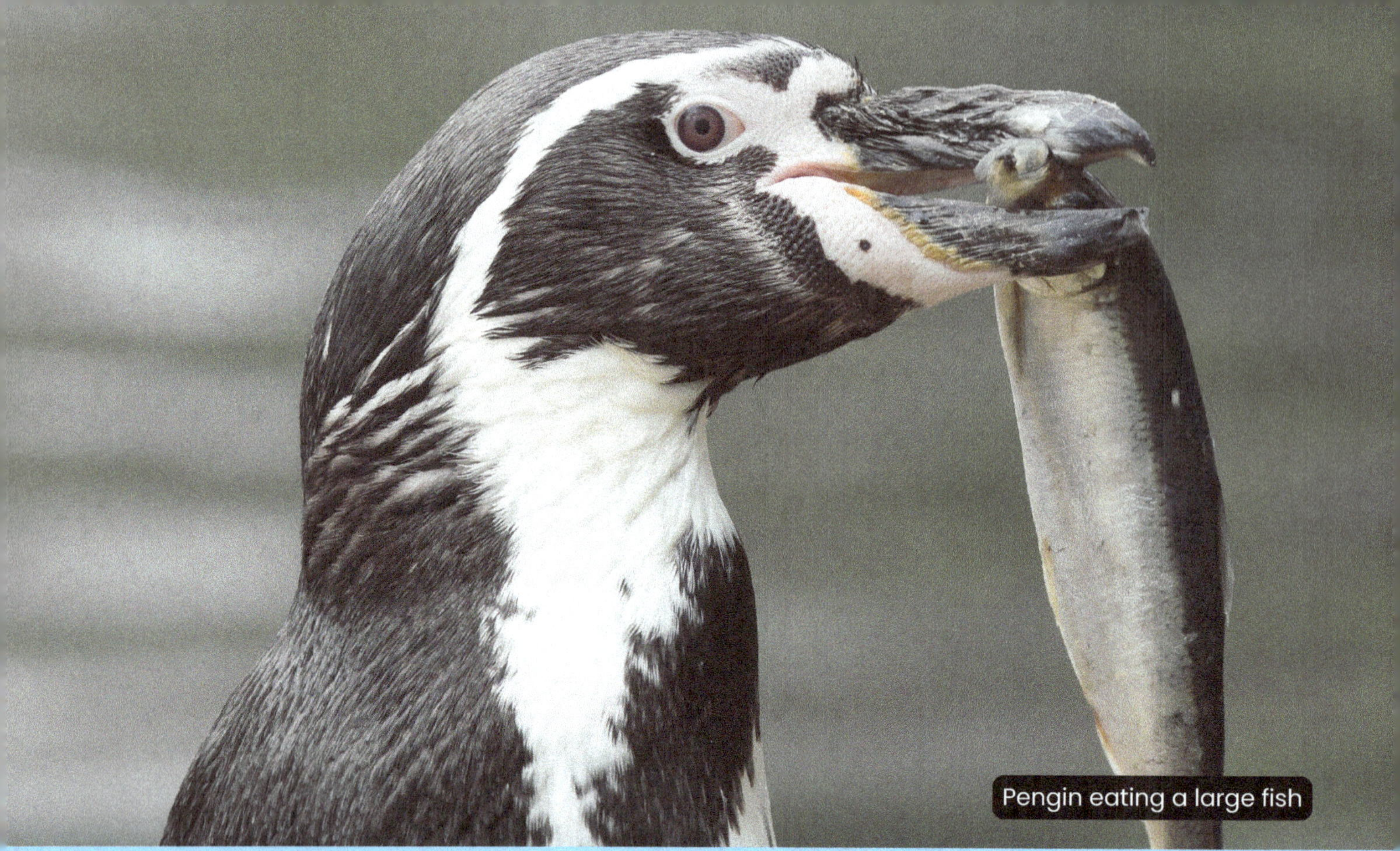

Pengin eating a large fish

Water birds such as ducks and flamingos may scoop up mouthfuls of water and mud, then strain out the food, like tiny plants, insects, or shrimp, using comb-like structures in their bills.

Birds of prey, also called raptors, such as hawks and eagles, use their powerful talons to catch animals and their hooked beaks to pull the meat into bite-sized pieces.

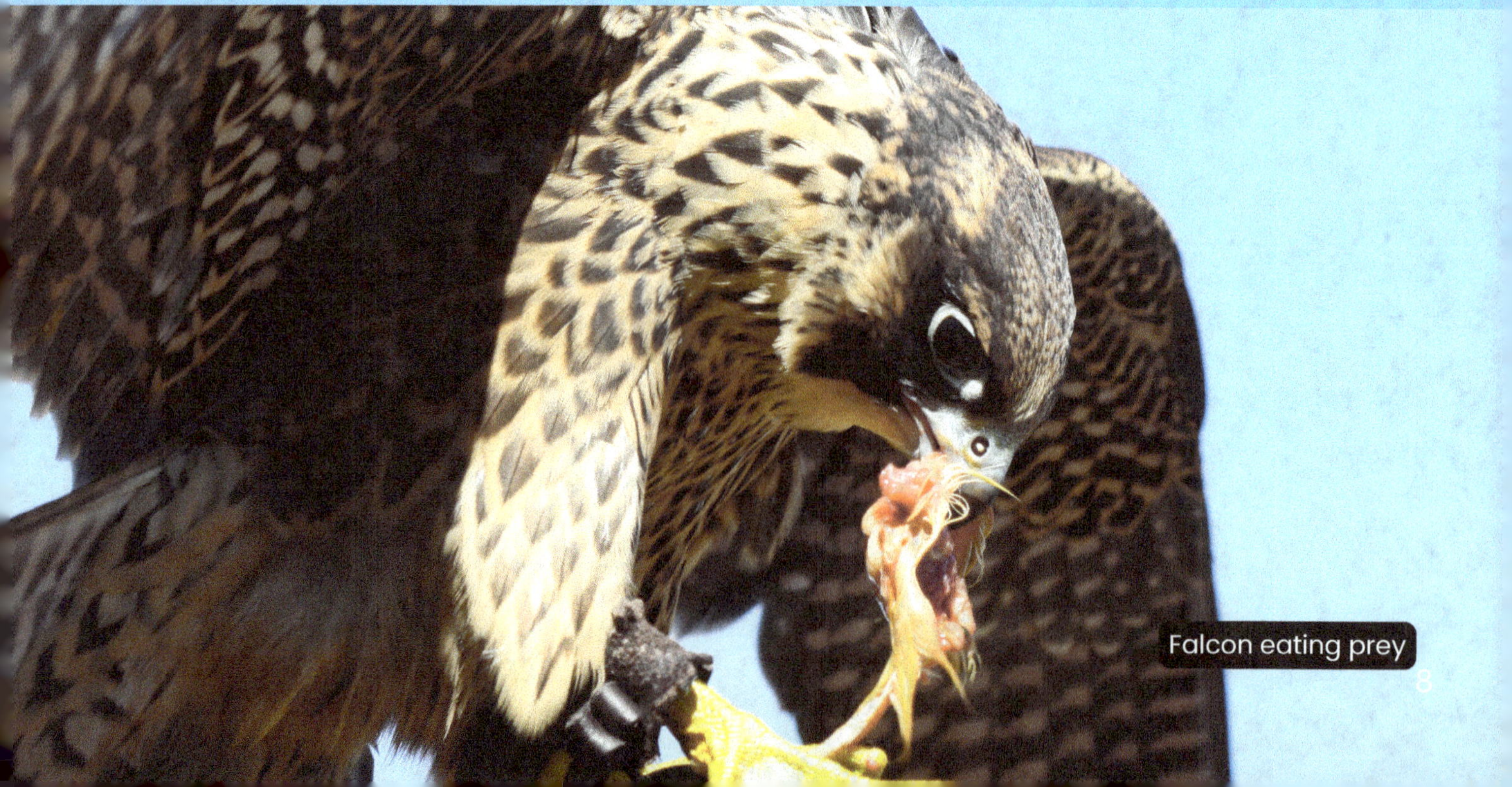

Falcon eating prey

HOW DO BIRDS MATE?

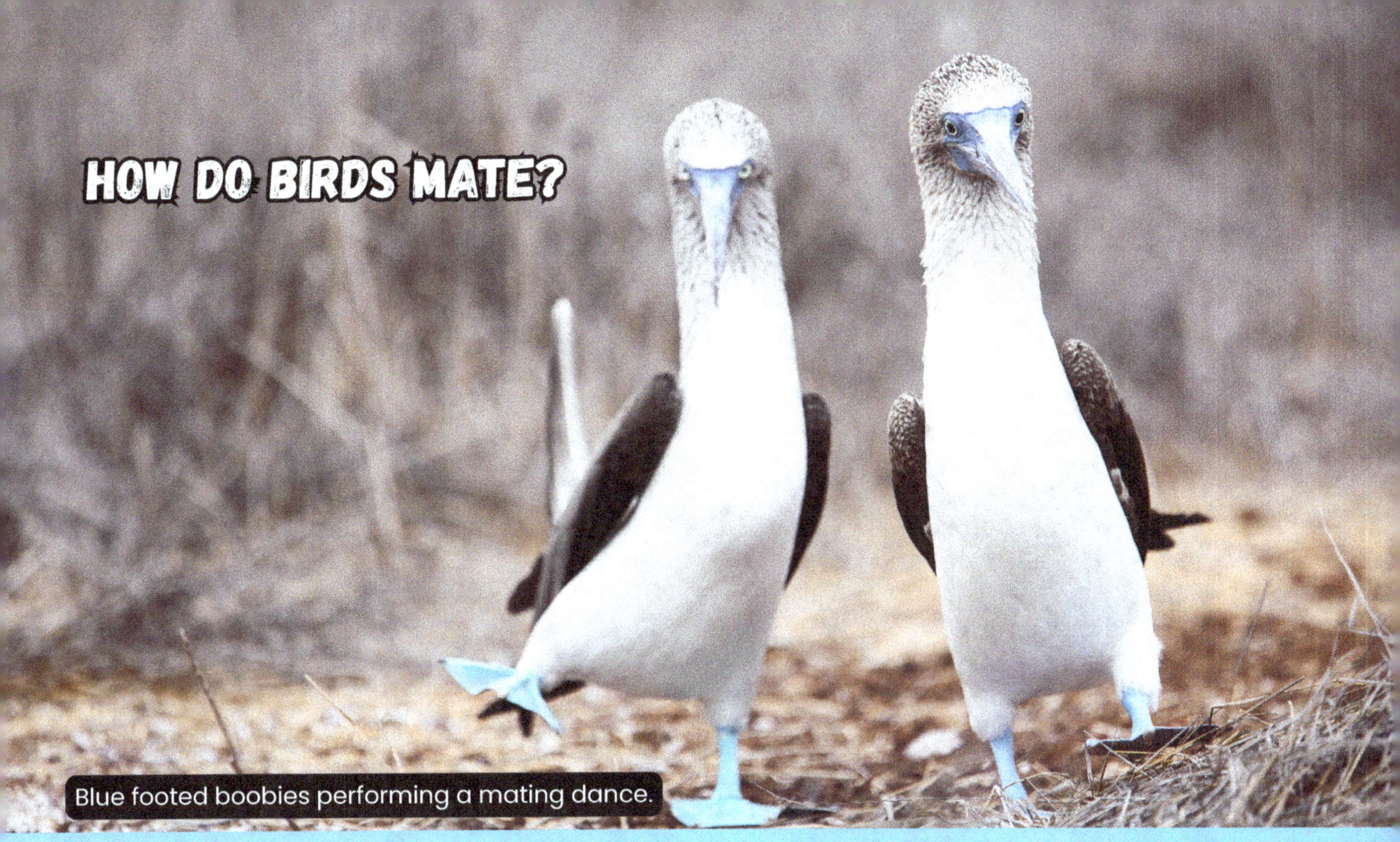
Blue footed boobies performing a mating dance.

When birds are ready to have babies, males and females go through a courtship period, where the males try to impress the females with songs, dances, or displays of bright feathers.

Many male birds sing loudly or perform dances or special moves, like hopping, bowing, or spreading their tails, to show a female that they are strong and healthy.

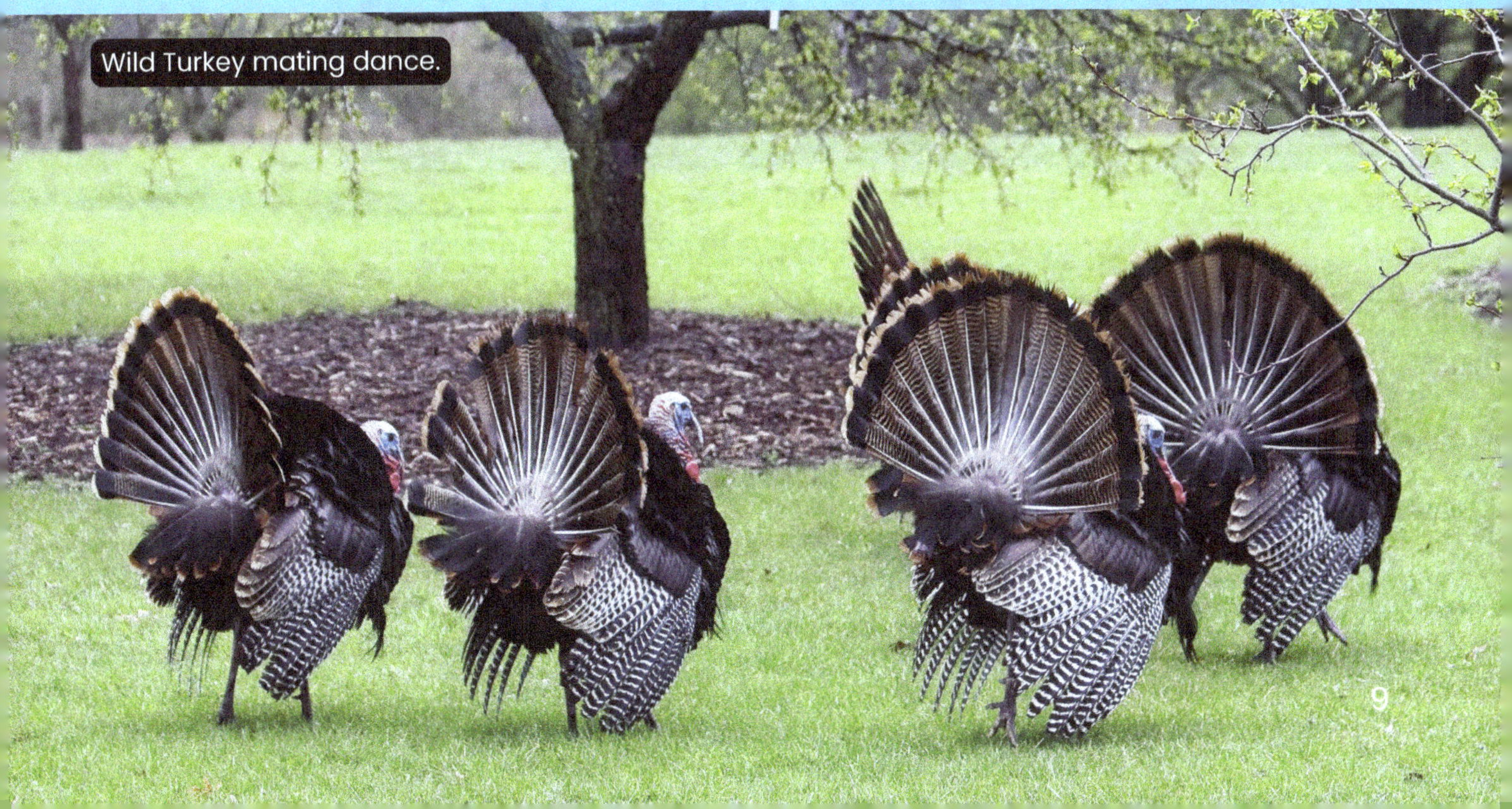
Wild Turkey mating dance.

A pair of swans

In many species, a male and female form a pair for at least one breeding season, and in some kinds of birds, like swans and ravens, the pair can stay together for life.

Carolina Wren

Most birds have a single opening under their tail called a cloaca, and during mating they briefly press these openings together in a "cloacal kiss" so the male can pass sperm to the female.

After mating, the female's body uses the sperm to fertilize her eggs, which then develop inside her before she lays them in a nest.

Hen with her egg

Birds usually choose nesting spots that help protect their eggs and baby birds, such as hidden tree branches, holes in trees, cliff ledges, or tall grass.

BABY BIRDS

Chicken hatching from egg

When a baby bird is still inside the egg, the parent birds must keep the eggs warm by sitting on them so the tiny baby bird can grow properly and be strong enough to hatch. When it is ready to hatch, it uses a special little bump on its beak, called an egg tooth, to crack the shell from the inside and slowly break its way out.

Although baby birds are commonly called chicks, not all bird species younglings are called that. For example, ducks have ducklings and eagles have eaglets and

Some baby birds, like ducklings and chicken chicks, hatch covered in soft down feathers and can walk, see, and follow their parents very soon after they leave the egg.

Chicken chick

Robin chick in nest

Sparrow chicks in nest

Ducklings

Other baby birds, like many songbirds, such as robins and sparrows, hatch naked or with only a few fuzzy feathers, their eyes are closed, and they must stay in the nest where their parents bring them food until they can fly out of their nests on their own.

Emperor penguins are famous for their parenting. After the female lays a single egg, the male balances it on his feet under a warm flap of skin while the female goes to feed.

Parent birds that raise nest babies have to work very hard to support them, flying back and forth many times a day with insects, worms, or other food to feed all the hungry, growing mouths.

Black Drongo feeding its chicks

In many bird species, both the mother and father share the jobs of chick care, taking turns keeping the chicks warm, watching for danger, and bringing food back to the nest.

BIRDS BIG & SMALL

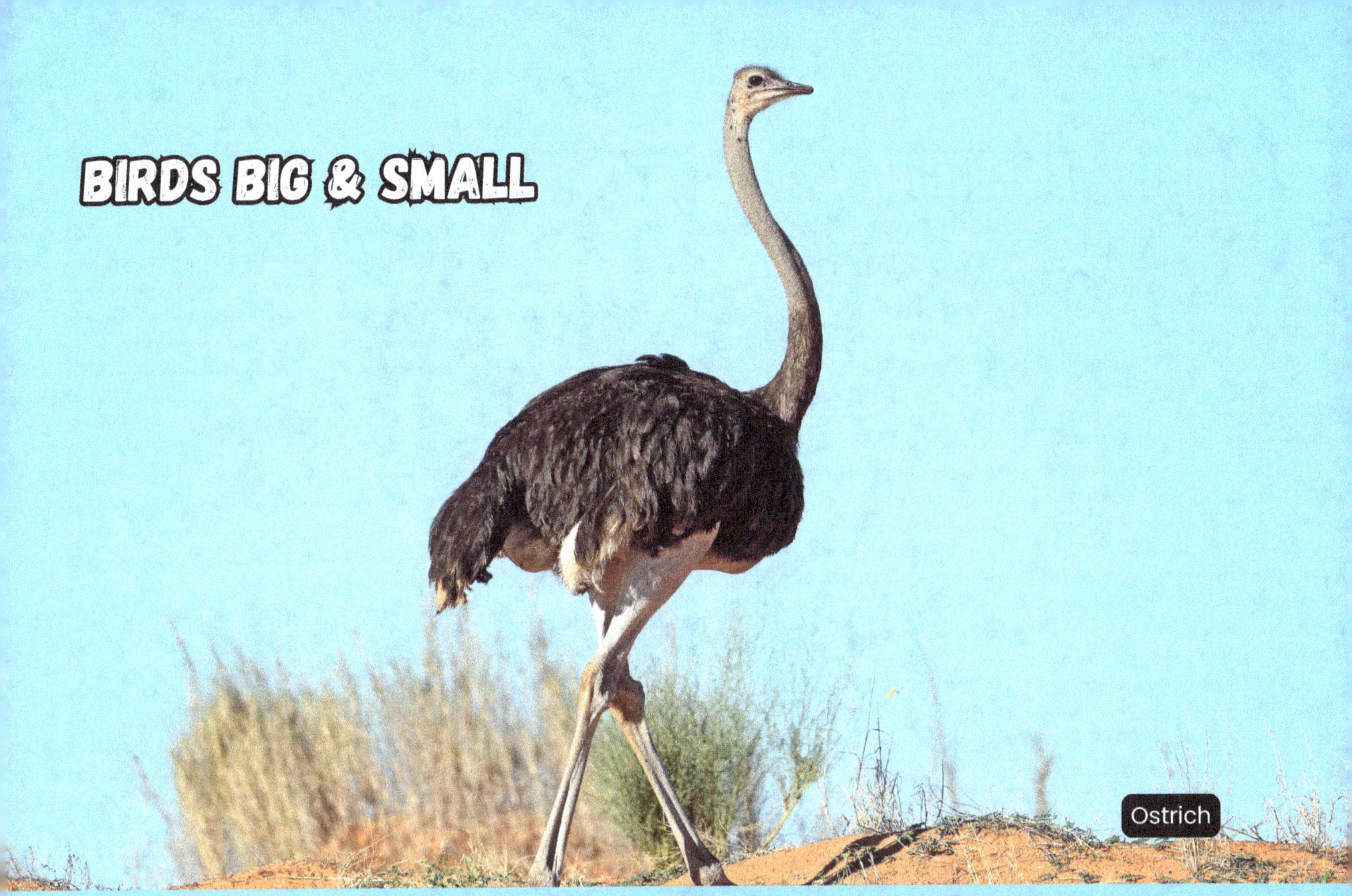

Ostrich

The ostrich is the world's largest living bird. It can be as tall as an adult human, sometimes even taller, reaching up to 8–9 feet/2.4–2.7 meters.

A native to the island of Cuba, the bee hummingbird is the smallest living bird. It's so tiny that it is about the size of a large bee and can weigh less than a penny.

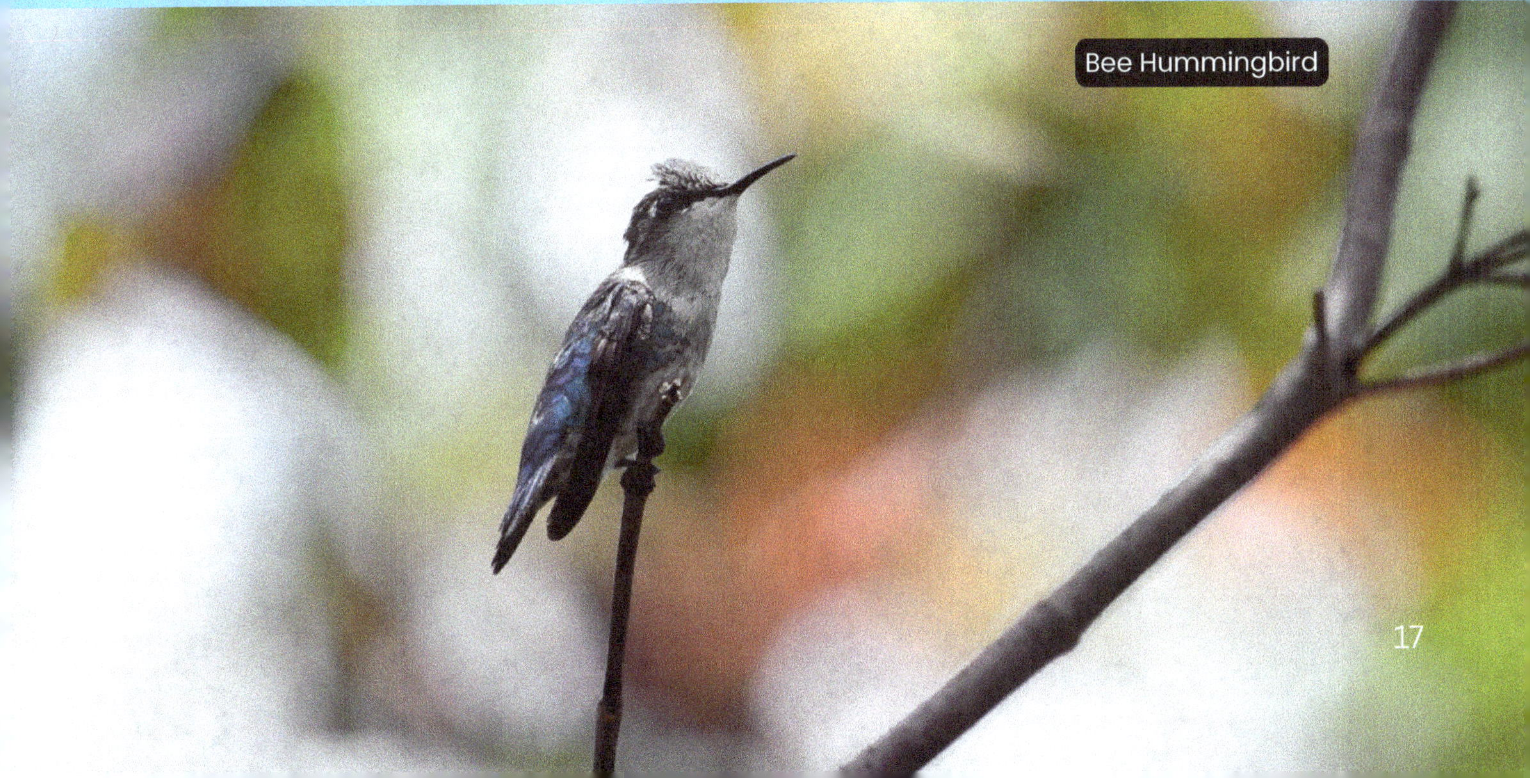

Bee Hummingbird

MEET THE BIRDS
Steller Jay

Sun Conure Parrots

BUDGIE OR PARAKEET
AUSTRALIA

Budgies are small parrots, usually the size of the length of a pen from the tip of their beak to the end of their tail, so they fit easily on your hand or shoulder.

Budgies can learn to copy human speech and whistles. Some can learn dozens of words if people talk to them often and practice with them.

Budgies are very social birds. They usually do better if they have another budgie or plenty of daily interaction with a human, so they don't get lonely or bored.

They use their beak almost like a third foot to climb around their cage, holding onto bars and toys while they move and play.

Cockatiels are small parrots from Australia with a special feather crest on top of their heads that rises when they are excited, curious, or startled, and flattens when they are calm.

They are known for whistling rather than talking. Many cockatiels can learn to whistle simple songs and copy sounds like doorbells or game noises.

In the wild, cockatiels live in flocks that roam open areas and stop at waterholes. Because of this, pet cockatiels usually enjoy having company and dislike being left alone for too long.

Cockatiels use gentle nibbling and preening to show affection. A tame bird may carefully preen your hair or clothes as if you are part of its flock.

Cockatiels can live 15–20 years or more with good care.

Canaries are small songbirds originally from islands called the Canary Islands, off the coast of Africa, where they lived in the wild long before people kept them as pets.

Male canaries are famous for their singing. They produce long, complex songs made from many different notes and trills, especially in the breeding season.

Canaries usually prefer not to be handled much. They are more like watch and listen pets that people enjoy hearing and seeing rather than cuddling.

A canary's song can change with its environment and health. If a male stops singing, it might be molting, stressed, or not feeling well.

They are very sensitive to air quality. In the past miners used canaries in coal mines as an early warning system for dangerous gases.

LOVEBIRD
AFRICA & ISLAND OF MADAGASCAR

Lovebirds are small, stocky parrots from Africa and nearby island of Madagascar. They are known for sitting close together and preening each other, which is how they got their name.

They are very active and curious. They like to chew, shred paper, and climb, so they need lots of safe toys and things to explore.

While they can learn a few sounds, they are not usually great talkers, most of their language is squeaks, chirps, and chatter.

In the wild, many species of lovebirds nest in tree cavities, carrying nesting material tucked in their feathers or beak back to their nest to make it comfortable.

Zebra Finch

Finches are tiny, lightweight birds that prefer to live in small groups or pairs, which is why they are often kept with at least one other finch.

The International Ornithological Committee (IOC) recognizes 238 species in the family of Fringillidae, which the IOC considers "true" finches.

Finches are better at flying than climbing, so they need a cage that is wider than it is tall, giving them room to fly from one side to the other.

American Gold Finch

Male finches sing to attract mates and mark their space. Their songs are usually a series of quick beeps, buzzes, and chirps.

Finches are usually too small and fast to be handled easily, so people mainly enjoy watching them build nests, preen, and interact with each other.

Red Brow Finch

Cockatoos are large parrots from Australia and nearby islands. They're known for their impressive feather crests and loud, attention getting calls.

They are extremely intelligent and emotional. They can learn tricks, solve puzzles, and show strong feelings like excitement, jealousy, or frustration.

Cockatoos often need several hours a day of interaction, play, and mental challenges to stay happy and avoid problem behaviors like loud screaming or feather plucking.

They can be very affectionate with people they trust, often wanting to cuddle, be petted, and sit close, but they can also be strong-beaked and must be handled respectfully.

Conure parrots are medium-sized parrots from Central and South America with bright, tropical colors. Many species have colors that are combinations of green, red, yellow, and blue.

They are very playful and clownish, often hanging upside down, rolling on their backs, and exploring everything with their beaks.

Conure parrots can be quite loud. Their high pitched calls can surprise people who don't realize how powerful a small parrot's voice can be.

They may learn a few words or short phrases, but they usually communicate more through body language and sounds than clear speech.

AFRICAN GREY PARROT
WEST & CENTRAL AFRICA

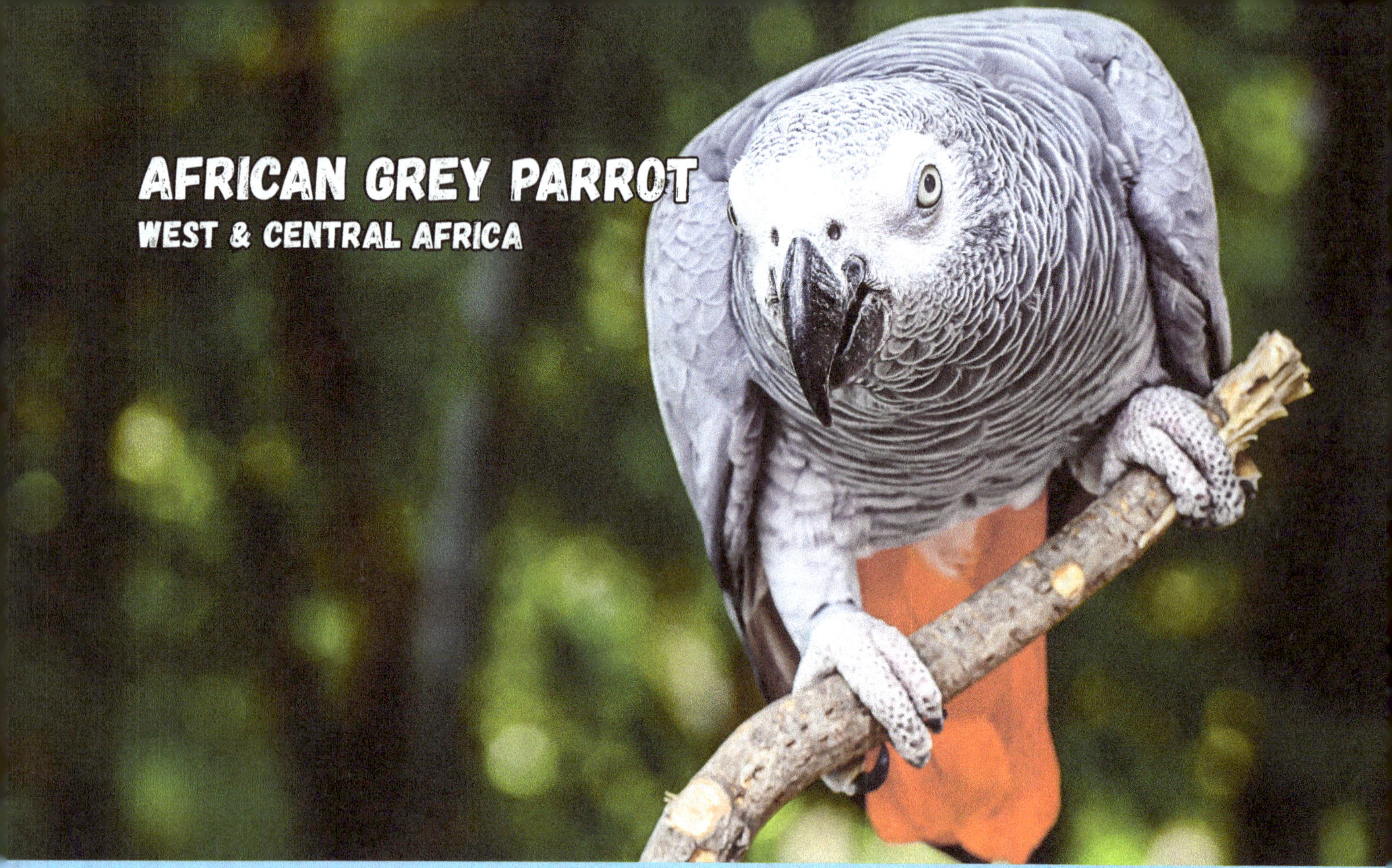

African grey parrots are considered some of the most intelligent birds. They can solve puzzles, remember many words, and sometimes use them in the right situations.

They are mostly grey with a bright red tail and pale face, giving them a very elegant and serious look compared to many colorful parrots.

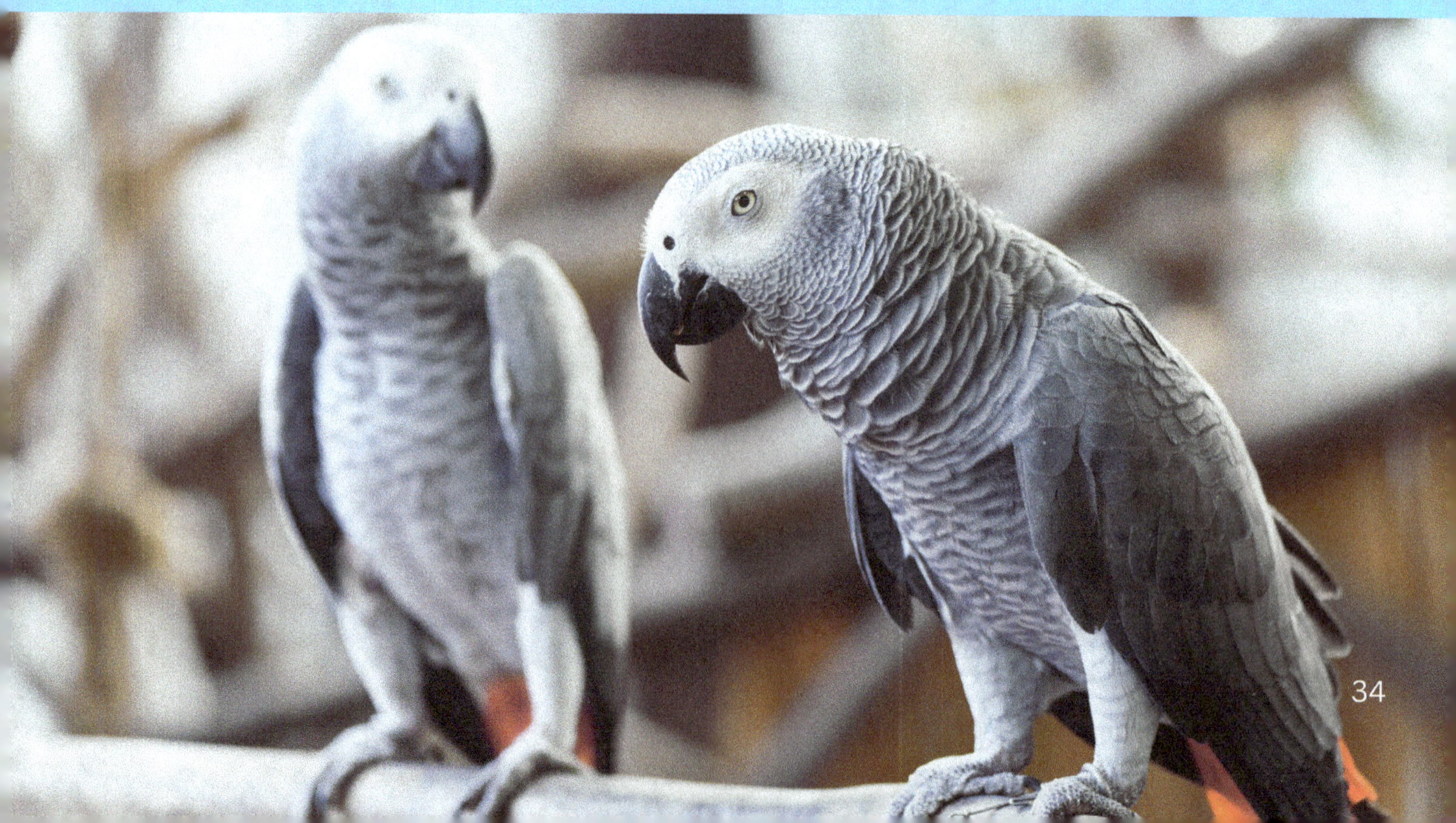

African greys are excellent mimics, copying not only human voices but also everyday sounds like microwaves, alarms, and even other pets.

They are sensitive and observant and may react strongly to changes in routine, new people, or stress in the household.

WILD BIRDS

Kingfisher

Osprey

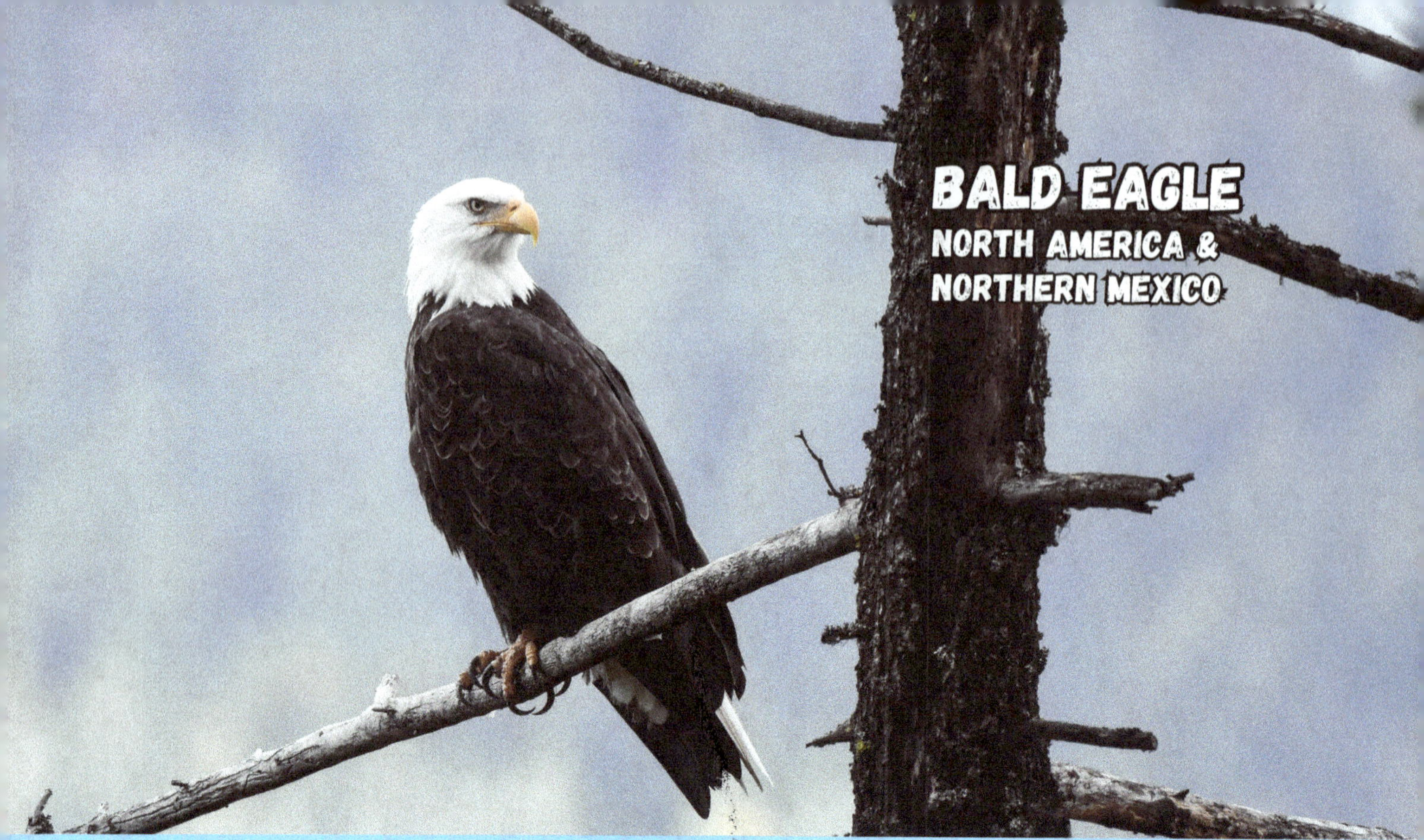

BALD EAGLE

NORTH AMERICA & NORTHERN MEXICO

The bald eagle is a large bird of prey. They can reach a height of 3 feet/.9 meters, a wingspan of up to 8 feet/2.4 meters, and weigh up to 15 pounds/6.8 kilograms.

Bald eagles are powerful fish hunters. They spot fish from high above and swoop down, grabbing them with strong, sharp talons. They sometimes steal food from other birds, like ospreys, by chasing them until the other bird drops its catch.

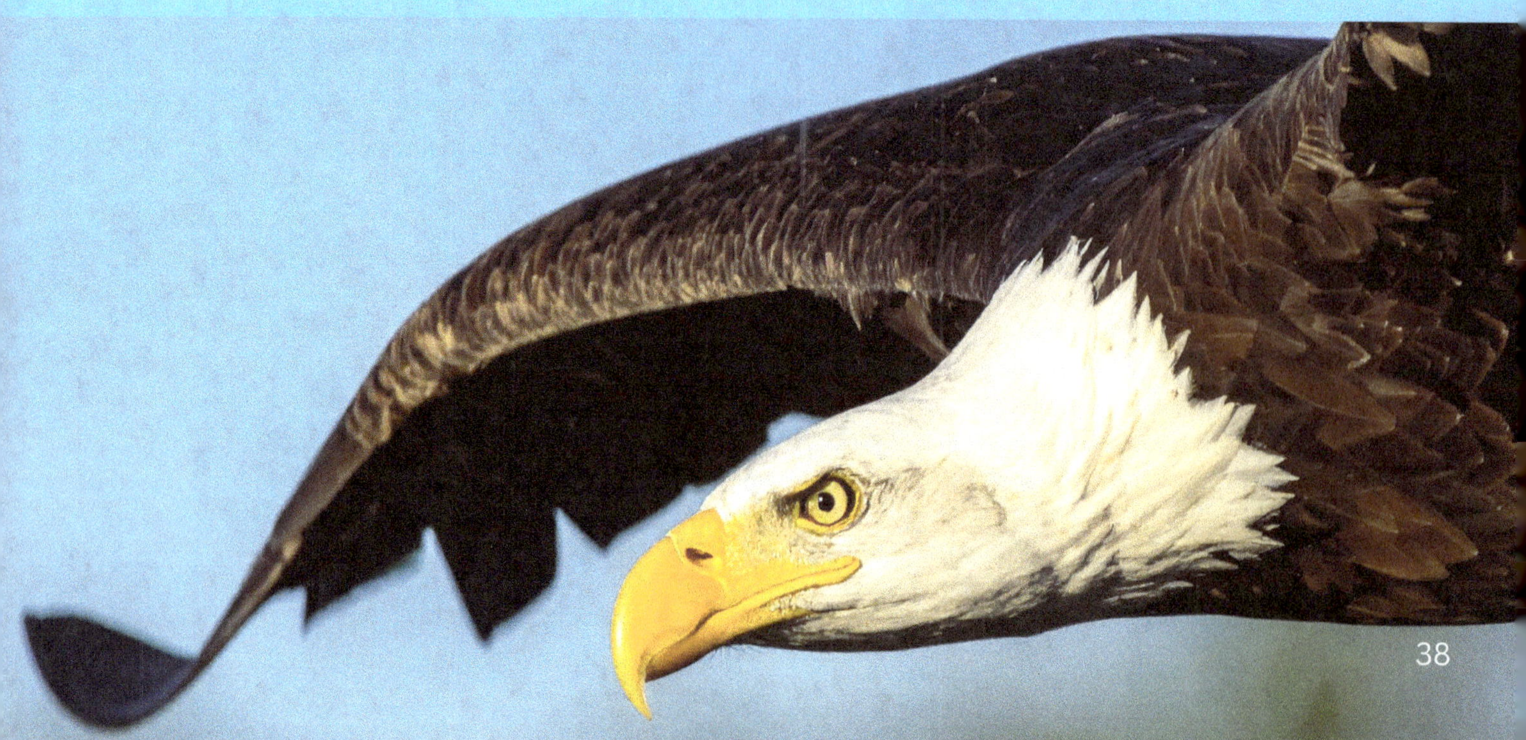

They build enormous nests called eyries in tall trees or on cliffs. A typical nest can be 5–6 feet/1.5-1.8 meters wide and 2–4 feet/.6-1.2 meters deep. They can weigh up to 4,400 pounds/1,996 kilograms, which is as much as a small car.

Adult bald eagles have a white head and tail with a dark brown body and wings, but young eagles are mottled brown and only get the white head after several years.

The bald eagle is the national symbol of the United States.

PEREGRINE FALCON
WORLDWIDE EXCEPT ANTARCTICA

Peregrine falcons are one of the most widespread raptors in the world.

They are famous for their diving speed. Their hunting dive is called a stoop, in which they can reach speeds over 200 miles per hour/89 meters per second, making them one of the fastest animals on Earth.

Peregrines mainly hunt other birds, hitting them in mid-air with closed talons to stun or kill them before catching them as they fall.

They have special adaptations for fast flight that include long, pointed wings, strong chest muscles, and bony structures in their nostrils to help them breathe at high speed.

Falconry is an ancient, special friendship where a person trains a wild bird, like a hawk or falcon, to be their hunting partner. Those who practice falconry, have partnered with peregrines for centuries.

Hummingbirds are tiny birds found in the Americas that flap their wings so fast, often 50 times per second or more, that they make a humming sound.

They can hover in mid-air, fly backwards, and change direction in an instant, which helps them drink nectar from flowers with great precision.

Hummingbirds have long, specialized tongues that flick in and out of a flower quickly to sip nectar. They also eat small insects for protein.

Their feathers can appear to shine with bright, metallic colors because of the way light reflects off special pancake shaped structures in thier feathers called melanosomes. These are stacked in a way that traps tiny air bubbles between them. When sunlight hits them, the light bends and bounces around making the light split into different colors in the feathers.

EMPEROR PENGUIN
ANTARCTICA

Emperor penguins are the tallest and heaviest penguins, living in Antarctica where temperatures and winds can be extremely harsh.

They cannot fly, but are designed to swim in the ocean. They use their strong flippers and streamlined bodies to help them reach speeds up to 6–7 mph/ 10–11 kph and bursts of up to 9–15 mph/ 14.4–22.5 kph.

During the long, dark Antarctic winter, male penguins huddle together in large groups to stay warm, taking turns standing on the cold outer edge.

Their black backs and white fronts help camouflage them from predators. From above, their dark backs blend with the deep water, and from below, their white bellies blend with the bright surface.

Barn owls have a heart-shaped facial disk that helps funnel sound into their ears, giving them extremely sharp hearing.

They hunt mostly at night and can find small animals, like mice, even in near total darkness because of their asymmetrical ears and unevenly placed ear holes. This adaptation allows sounds from above or below to reach each ear at slightly different times and intensities, allowing the owl to pinpoint vertical and horizontal locations.

Their feathers are designed for silent flight. The edges of the wings are soft and fringed, which reduces the sound of air moving over them.

To look around, an owl can twist its neck a long way, up to about 270 degrees, but it can't spin its head all the way around.

After eating small animals, owls cough up pellets made of fur, bones, and other parts they can't digest. Scientists and students can study these pellets to learn what the owl was eating.

WOODPECKER
MOST FORESTED REGIONS IN THE WORLD

Woodpeckers use their strong, chisel-like beaks to drill into wood to find insects, build nest cavities, and communicate.

They have very tough skulls and special shock absorbing structures in their heads to protect their brains. These include a hyoid apparatus that wraps all the way around the back of their skull and acts like a seatbelt for their brain, a spongy bone armor, and a brain that fits snuggly in their skull.

Many woodpeckers have long, sticky tongues that can stretch far out of their beaks to reach insects deep inside holes and cracks.

Their feet usually have two toes facing forward and two facing backward, which helps them cling to vertical tree trunks.

Different species drum at different speeds and rhythms, which can act like a signature to other woodpeckers in the area.

Pigeons are common in cities around the world, but their wild ancestors originally lived on rocky cliffs in Europe, North Africa, and western Asia.

They are believed to be the first bird domesticated by humans, with evidence dating back more than 5,000 years ago.

They have an impressive homing ability and can find their way back to their home loft from long distances, which is why people once used them as message carriers.

They feed on seeds, grains, and human scraps, which is why they are often seen pecking around parks, sidewalks, and train stations.

Pigeons have excellent vision and can see patterns and colors well. They are even used in some experiments to study how animals recognize images.

Albatrosses are large seabirds that spend most of their lives flying over the open ocean, far away from land.

Some albatross species have wingspans over 10 feet/3 meters, making them among the birds with the largest wings on Earth.

They are expert gliders. They use ocean winds to soar for hours without flapping their wings much, saving energy on long journeys.

They feed mostly on fish and squid, often following ships or feeding near areas where underwater currents bring food close to the surface.

Albatrosses can travel huge distances across the ocean in a single year, crossing thousands of miles/kilometers as they search for food and return to their nesting sites.

Ravens are among the smartest birds and can solve puzzles, use tools like sticks to get food, and even play games with each other.

They do flips, rolls, and barrel rolls in the air, sometimes flying upside down for over half a mile just to show off.

Ravens usually pair up with one mate for life and do fancy aerial dances together during courtship.

While breeding pairs defend territory alone, young ravens form big winter flocks and work together to find food. Although there are other names for this grouping, it is most commonly called an unkndness of ravens.

Ravens can remember human faces for years and hold grudges against people who bothered them.

BIRD WONDERS

Robin

Every bird has its own song voice. Even when two birds are the same kind, their songs can sound a little different, almost like how people have different voices and ways of talking.

Feathers are found only on birds. Lots of animals have fur or scales, but only birds grow feathers, which help them fly, stay warm, and show off beautiful colors and patterns.

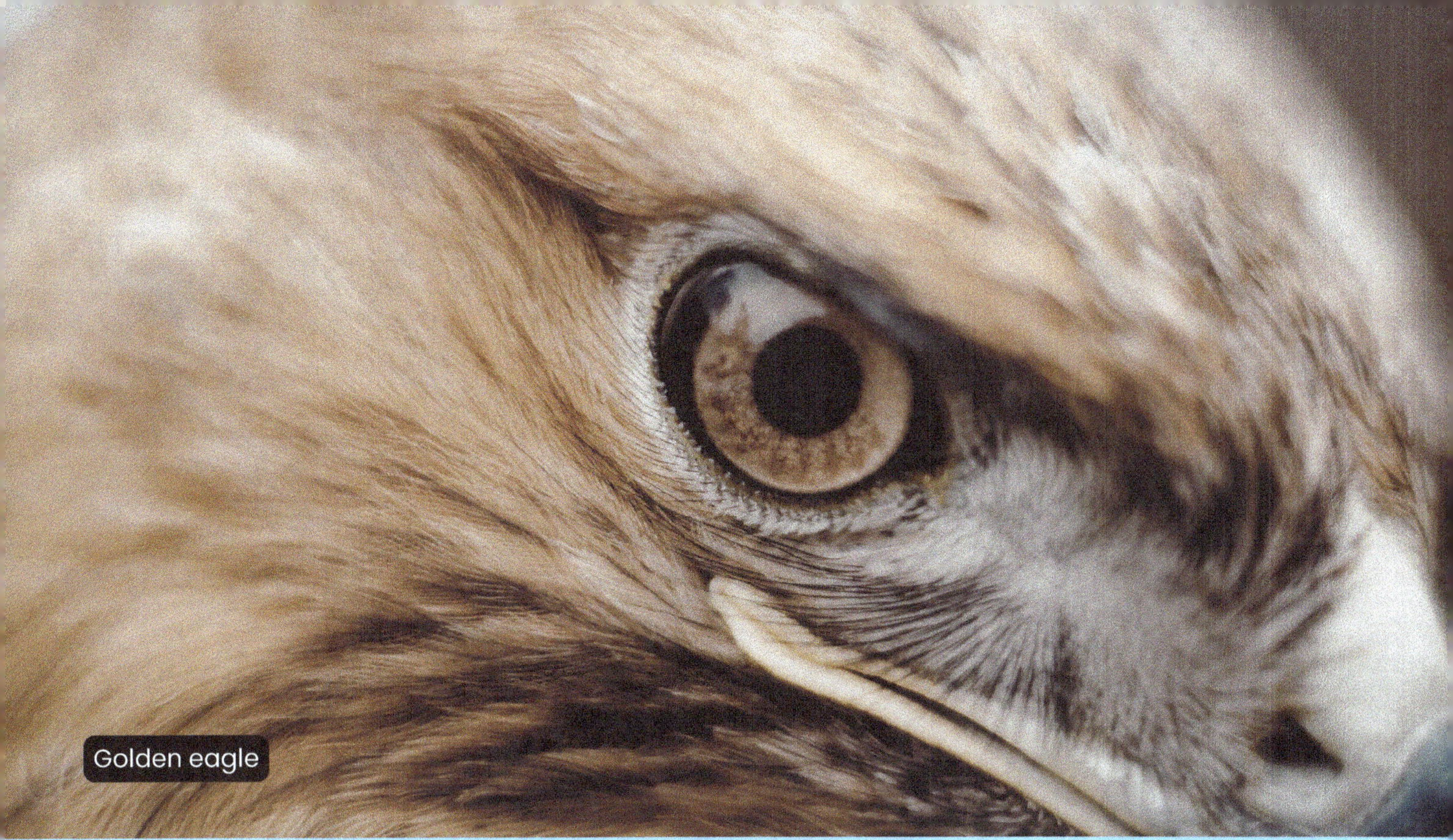
Golden eagle

Many birds see colors we can't see. Their eyes can see ultraviolet (UV) light, a spectrum invisible to humans, becuase of this a bird looking at another bird's feathers may see patterns that human eyes miss.

Some birds can sleep while they're flying. Certain birds that travel long distances over the ocean can rest half of their brain at a time, so they can keep flying and not fall from the sky.

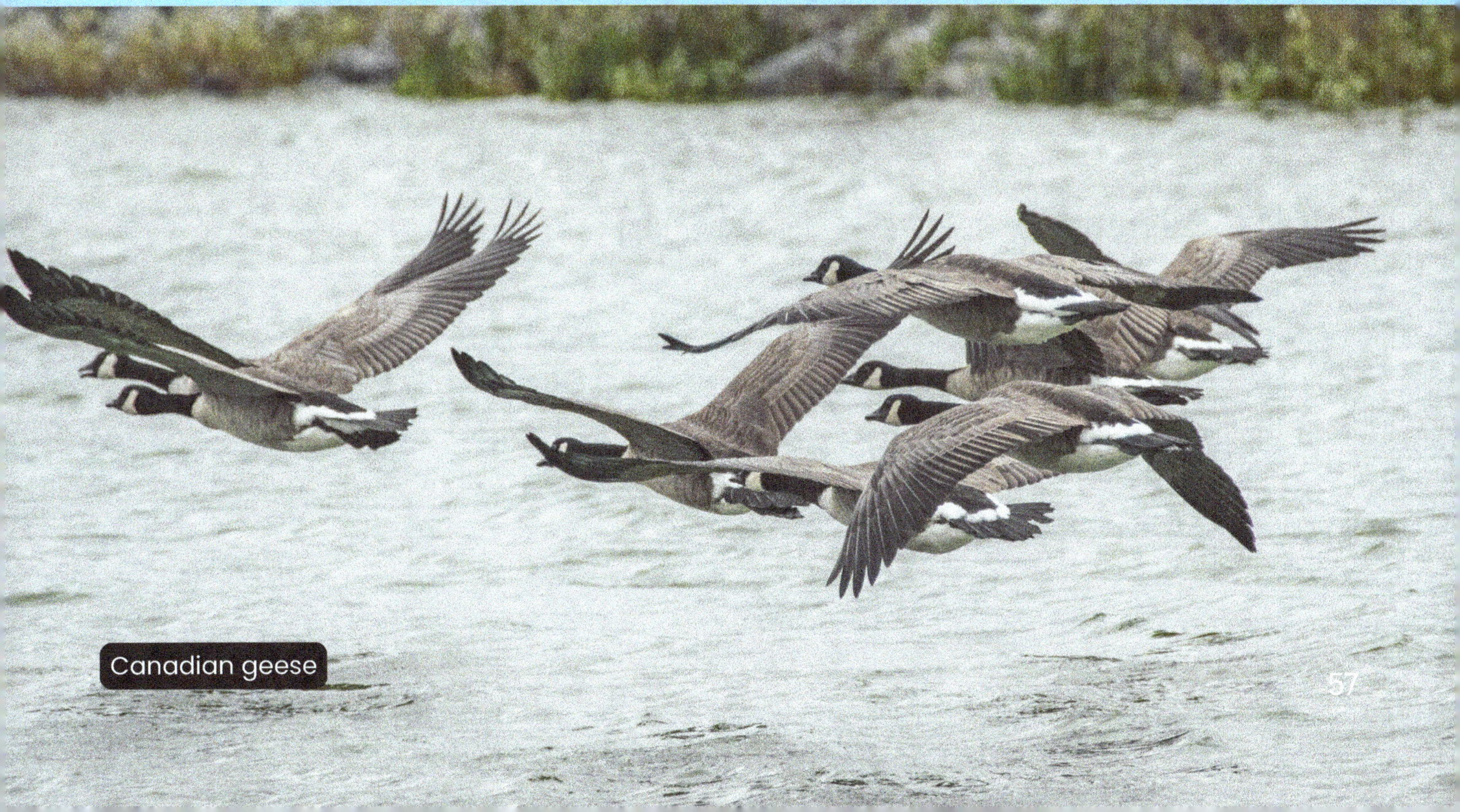
Canadian geese

Sun conure parrots

Some parrots think phones are funny. They sometimes copy ringtone sounds or pretend to answer the phone by saying things like, "Hello?" when they hear people talking.

Certain shorebirds fake an "ouch" to trick predators. A parent bird may pretend to have a hurt wing and wobble away so the predator follows them and not the nest.

Crows and ravens play games. They have been seen sliding down snowy roofs, playing drop-and-catch with sticks, and even teasing other animals, almost like they're having recess.

Seagull

Some seagulls use bread to bait fish. They drop a piece of bread on the water and wait for a fish to come up to nibble it, then quickly grab the fish instead of the bread.

Some birds like Clark's nutcrackers and jays hide food for later. They hide seeds and nuts in hundreds of little spots and can remember many of those hiding places months later.

Clark's nutcracker

Rooks playing in the snow

Rooks and crows sometimes prank each other. They have been seen pulling another bird's tail or stealing its food and then flying just out of reach, almost like a teasing game.

Crows

Uilleum the Dodo gives Alice her own thimble for winning the Caucus-race.

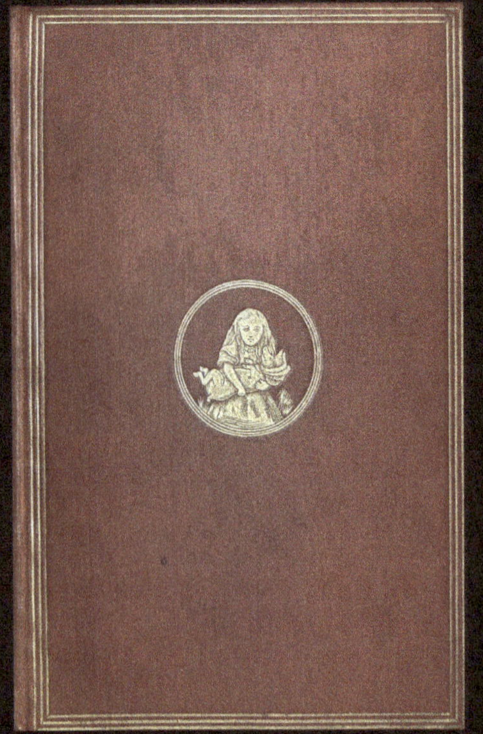

Uilleam the Dodo is a minor character in Lewis Carroll's 1865 classic novel **Alice's Adventures in Wonderland**. He's one of the first animals that Alice talks to when she enters Wonderland in her pool of tears. It's the Dodo's idea that all the animals who almost drown in her pool of tears have a Caucas-race in order to dry themselves off. When the race was done, he declared Alice the winner and presented her with her own thimble as her prize.

The famous author and poet Edgar Allen Poe's poem, The Raven, was first published in 1845. The poem turned Edgar Allen Poe into an instant celebrity of the time, and, transformed the raven into an iconic symbol of gothic horror, inescapable grief, and madness in modern culture.

Stay quiet and move slowly. Birds can scare easily, so walk gently, keep your voice soft, and avoid sudden movements so they feel safe.

Give birds personal space. Watch from a distance and don't try to touch them. If they hop or fly away from you, you are too close and should take a step back.

Never bother nests, eggs, or baby birds. Even if they look cute or alone, don't touch or poke around nests, because parents may get scared and stay away.

Do not feed birds people food. Bread, chips, and junk food can make birds sick. It's better to let them find their own natural food or use proper bird seed with an adult's help.

Watch where you walk and look around. Stay on paths, be careful not to step on small birds or their hiding places, and be aware of things like water, holes, or branches so you stay safe too.

THE LEGEND OF THE PHOENIX

The phoenix is a legendary, eagle-sized bird with brilliant scarlet and gold plumage that lives for hundreds of years. At the end of its life, it builds a nest of aromatic spices, sets it on fire, and is consumed in the flames, only to rise again, reborn and renewed from the ashes.

The earliest stories of the Phoenix come from ancient Egyptian mythology. It was inspired by the bennu bird, an African heron that Egyptians associated with Ra, the sun god, and Osiris, the god of the underworld. The bennu was also associated with the seasonal flooding in the Nile Valley.

The symbol of suffering and rebrith was adopted by many traditions throughout history including the Greeks, the Romans, Christians, and is a popular figure in Western art and literature.

BONUS ACTIVITY PAGES

Fun activities to keep exploring the amazing world of birds!

Bird
WORD SEARCH

HUMMINGBIRD
ALBATROSS
WINGSPAN
RAVEN
CANARY
EGGS
CHICK
EAGLE
NEST

L	N	V	F	O	Y	H	Q	A	D	L	M	T	W
I	A	Q	A	L	B	A	T	R	O	S	S	M	Z
P	V	V	Z	M	N	E	P	A	S	D	H	P	H
S	N	Z	Q	W	H	Z	E	K	E	Q	N	U	R
G	U	K	Q	P	B	U	G	V	C	A	M	C	O
G	T	F	O	A	B	F	K	K	P	M	R	H	U
E	R	P	V	C	P	G	P	S	I	D	P	I	Z
U	V	Z	S	U	A	W	G	N	M	C	L	C	A
U	C	J	V	Y	D	N	G	G	E	B	U	K	W
O	W	D	E	Z	I	B	A	P	K	V	F	H	S
I	F	B	L	W	I	O	T	R	T	F	A	P	N
N	P	V	P	R	S	O	W	S	Y	A	E	R	K
K	G	P	D	O	E	W	E	Q	K	Q	P	Q	P
Y	W	P	V	O	N	N	E	L	G	A	E	V	W

Bird
WORD SCRAMBLE

Unscramble the following words

R O T S H I C

____

G N U M H I B R D I M

____

H F E A T R E S

____

Z I G Z A R D

____

I G I D U B E

____

E W O D P E C K O E R

____

C O N F A L

____

T S E N

____

R E T S C

____

C A L O C A

____

Bird CROSSWORD

Across:

2. The special body covering that helps birds fly
3. A safe place that a bird builds to lay eggs and raise chicks
5. These animals have been around since the time of the dinosaurs
6. Some birds can copy this, along with other sounds
10. Bird sounds that can be chirps, whistles, or squawks

Down:

1. Birds sometimes travel across these huge areas of land
2. Place where many birds live together among the trees
4. You might hear birds doing this in your backyard trees
5. Part of a bird's body used for pecking and picking up food
7. Tiny bird that can hover and flap its wings very fast
8. Very large bird of prey with powerful wings and sharp talons
9. Extremely fast bird known for its speed in the air

Bird MATCH

Match the bird to its home.

Bird QUIZ

True or False?

1. Birds are the only animals that have feathers on their bodies. True or False?
2. Budgies and other parrots use their beaks almost like an extra foot to help them climb around their cages. True or False?
3. The bee hummingbird is one of the smallest birds, and it can be about the size of a large bee. True or False?
4. In many bird species, both the mother and father help take care of the eggs and chicks, sharing jobs like keeping them warm and bringing food. True or False?
5. All chicks stay helpless in the nest for a long time after hatching and cannot walk right away. True or False?
6. Hummingbirds can hover in place and even fly backward while they drink nectar from flowers. True or False?
7. Birds do not have teeth, so they use a special organ called a gizzard to help grind up their food inside their bodies. True or False?
8. Penguins are birds that can swim very well but cannot fly in the air. True or False?
9. Peregrine falcons are very slow fliers and mostly walk to catch their food. True or False?
10. Some birds store or hide extra food, like seeds and nuts, and can remember many of the places where they hid them. True or False?

Bird MULTIPLE CHOICE

Pick the best answer from what you've read..

1. Scientists think modern birds are closely related to which ancient animals?
   A. Early fish
   B. Reptile dinosaurs
   C. Giant insects
   D. Early mammals
2. Which bird is the biggest living bird on Earth today?
   A. Bald eagle
   B. Ostrich
   C. Albatross
   D. Emperor penguin
3. Which bird is known for being one of the smallest and about the size of a large bee?
   A. Canary
   B. Bee hummingbird
   C. Pigeon
   D. Cockatiel
4. What special thing can many parrots, like budgies and African greys, do?
   A. Glow in the dark
   B. Change color like chameleons
   C. Copy human words and sounds
   D. Sleep all winter
5. What is the main reason feathers are unique to birds?
   A. Only birds have feathers
   B. Only birds have fur
   C. Only birds have scales
   D. Only birds have shells

Bird MULTIPLE CHOICE

Pick the best answer from what you've read.

6. What do many male birds do during courtship to impress a female?
   A. Hide in the nest quietly
   B. Sing songs and perform dances
   C. Sleep until she chooses them
   D. Break their own eggs
7. What do birds use instead of teeth to help grind up their food inside their bodies?
   A. Feathers
   B. Gizzard
   C. Cloaca
   D. Air sacs
8. Which statement about chicks is true?
   A. All chicks stay helpless in the nest for months.
   B. Ducklings and chicken chicks can often walk and follow a parent soon after hatching.
   C. No chicks need their parents after they hatch.
   D. All chicks can fly on the day they hatch.
9. What is special about a peregrine falcon when it hunts?
   A. It swims underwater to catch fish.
   B. It walks quietly through the grass.
   C. It dives at very high speeds to catch other birds in the air.
   D. It only eats seeds it finds on the ground.
10. What do some birds, like jays and nutcrackers, do with extra seeds and nuts?
    A. Throw them away so other birds can't eat them.
    B. Hide them in many places to eat later.
    C. Drop them into rivers so they float away.
    D. Feed them to predators to distract them.

MY FAVORITE

FAVORITE

Write or draw your favorite bird below

Bird
STORY

Imagine you have a pet bird, or maybe you have one of your own. What is his/her name? Where does your bird live? What does he/she eat? What are they afraid of? Write a story in the space provided below about your pet bird.

____

____

____

____

____

____

____

____

____

____

____

____

____

____

____

By: _______________________________

Bird

COLORING

PAGES

Peacock

Chickadee

Barn Owl

Bald Eagle

Flamingo

American Goldfinch

Cockatoo

Peregren Falcon

Blue Jay

Hummingbird

Answers

Bird
WORD SEARCH

HUMMINGBIRD
ALBATROSS
WINGSPAN
RAVEN
CANARY
EGGS
CHICK
EAGLE
NEST

L	N	V	F	O	Y	H	Q	A	D	L	M	T	W
I	A	Q	A	L	B	A	T	R	O	S	S	M	Z
P	V	V	Z	M	N	E	P	A	S	D	H	P	H
S	N	Z	Q	W	H	Z	E	K	E	Q	N	U	R
G	U	K	Q	P	B	U	G	V	C	A	M	C	O
G	T	F	O	A	B	F	K	K	P	M	R	H	U
E	R	P	V	C	P	G	P	S	I	D	P	I	Z
U	V	Z	S	U	A	W	G	N	M	C	L	C	A
U	C	J	V	Y	D	N	G	G	E	B	U	K	W
O	W	D	E	Z	I	B	A	P	K	V	F	H	S
I	F	B	L	W	I	O	T	R	T	F	A	P	N
N	P	V	P	R	S	O	W	S	Y	A	E	R	K
K	G	P	D	O	E	W	E	Q	K	Q	P	Q	P
Y	W	P	V	O	N	N	E	L	G	A	E	V	W

Bird
WORD SCRAMBLE

ROTSHIC   OSTRICH

GNUMHIBRDIM   HUMMINGBIRD

HFEATRES   FEATHERS

ZIGZARD   GIZZARD

IGIDUBE   BUDGIE

EWODPECKOER   WOODPECKER

CONFAL   FALCON

TSEN   NEST

RETSC   CREST

CALOCA   CLOACA

Bird CROSSWORD

Across:

2. The special body covering that helps birds fly
3. A safe place that a bird builds to lay eggs and raise chicks
5. These animals have been around since the time of the dinosaurs
6. Some birds can copy this, along with other sounds
10. Bird sounds that can be chirps, whistles, or squawks

Down:

1. Birds sometimes travel across these huge areas of land
2. Place where many birds live together among the trees
4. You might hear birds doing this in your backyard trees
5. Part of a bird's body used for pecking and picking up food
7. Tiny bird that can hover and flap its wings very fast
8. Very large bird of prey with powerful wings and sharp talons
9. Extremely fast bird known for its speed in the air

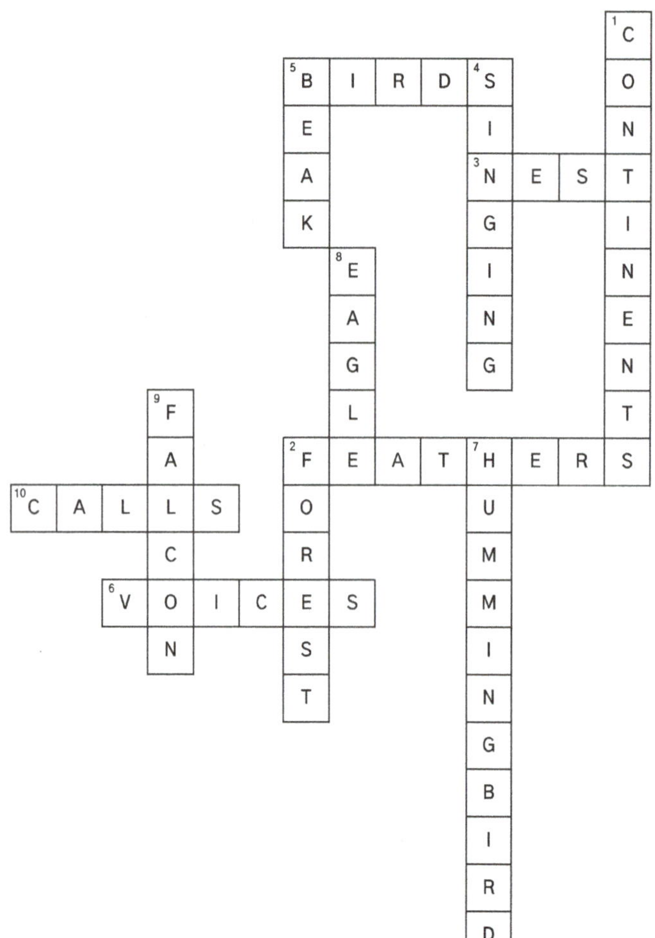

Bird MATCH

Match the bird to its home.

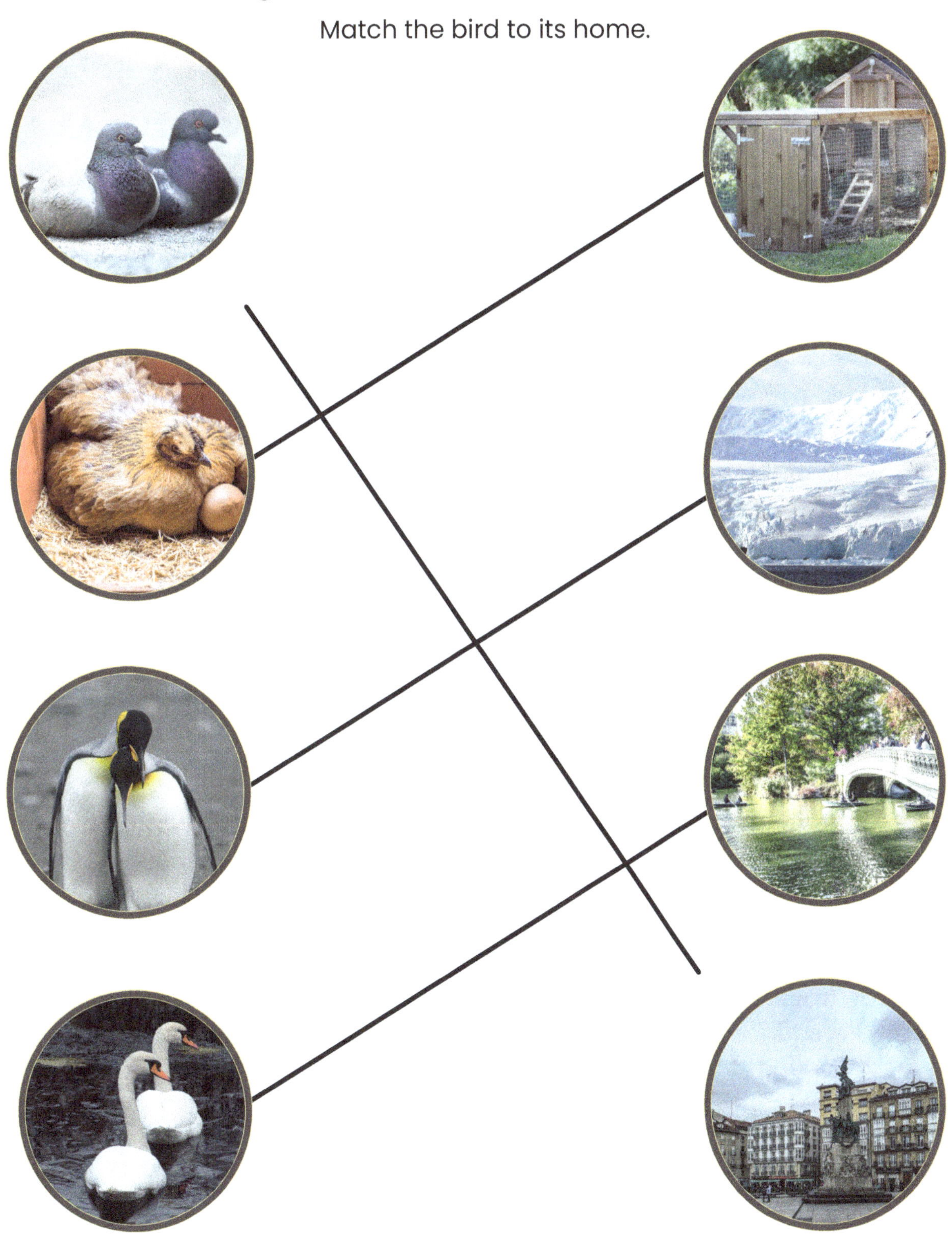

Bird QUIZ

1. True - Birds are the only animals that grow feathers, other animals have fur, hair, or scales, but not feathers.
2. True - Parrots like budgies often use their beaks to grip bars and toys, almost like a third foot, to help them climb.
3. True - The bee hummingbird is one of the world's smallest birds and can be about the size of a large bee and lighter than a penny.
4. True - In many species, both parents share the work. They take turns warming eggs, feeding chicks, and watching for danger.
5. False - Some chicks, like ducklings and chicken chicks, can walk and follow a parent soon after hatching, while songbird chicks often stay helpless in the nest.
6. True - Hummingbirds can hover in one spot and even fly backward, which helps them drink nectar from flowers.
7. True - Birds have no teeth, so a strong organ called the gizzard grinds up their food, often with the help of swallowed grit or tiny stones.
8. True - Penguins are birds that cannot fly in the air but are excellent swimmers, they can travel through the water at high speeds with their flipper-like wings.
9. False - Peregrine falcons are among the fastest animals on Earth. They dive at very high speeds to catch other birds in mid-air.
10. True - Some birds, such as certain crows and jays, store food like seeds and nuts in many hiding places and can remember where a lot of them are later.

Bird MULTIPLE CHOICE

1. B. Reptile dinosaurs - Birds evolved from feathered dinosaurs, sharing traits like laying eggs with hard shells and similar hip bones.
2. B. Ostrich - The ostrich is the biggest living bird, as tall as a human adult and lays very large eggs.
3. B. Bee hummingbird - The bee hummingbird is one of the smallest birds, about the size of a large bee and lighter than a penny.
4. C. Copy human words and sounds - Parrots like budgies and African greys are famous for mimicking human speech, whistles, and everyday sounds.
5. A. Only birds have feathers - Feathers are unique to birds; other animals have fur, scales, or hair, but never feathers.
6. B. Sing songs and perform dances - Male birds impress females during courtship with songs, dances, bowing, or showing off feathers. B. Gizzard - Birds have no teeth, so their gizzard (a strong stomach muscle) grinds food, often using swallowed grit.
7. B. Ducklings and chicken chicks can often walk and follow a parent soon after hatching - Ground-nesting chicks like ducks and chickens hatch ready to walk, unlike helpless nest songbird chicks.
8. C. It dives at very high speeds to catch other birds in the air - Peregrine falcons dive over 200 mph to hunt other birds mid-air, making them one of the fastest animals.
9. B. Hide them in many places to eat later - Birds like jays, crows, and nutcrackers store seeds/nuts in hundreds of spots and remember the locations.
10. B. Hide them in many places to eat later - Birds like jays, crows, and nutcrackers store seeds/nuts in hundreds of spots and remember the locations.